G000089504

Quick Revision

KS3

English

Ron Simpson

First published 2007
exclusively for WHSmith by
Hodder Education, part of Hachette Livre UK,
338 Euston Road
London
NW1 3BH

Impression number   10 9 8 7 6 5 4 3 2
Year   2010 2009 2008

A CIP record for this book is available from the British Library.

The right of Ron Simpson to be identified as the author of this work has been asserted by him.

Cover illustration by Sally Newton Illustrations.

Typeset by Starfish Design Editorial and Project Management Ltd.

ISBN: 978 0 340 94307 6

Printed and bound in the UK by Hobbs the Printers Ltd.

Adjectives and adverbs

Before you try to understand what adjectives and adverbs are, make sure that you know about nouns and verbs. If you have any doubts, look up those sections now. You might have learned that adjectives are 'describing words'. This can be a helpful definition, but it is only partly true.
- **Adjectives** give us more information about nouns (or pronouns).
- **Adverbs** give us more information about verbs.

This information is sometimes descriptive, but not always. Look at the following uses of adjectives: 'a *good* teacher'/'our *next* teacher', 'a *brilliant* goal'/'the *second* goal', 'an *exciting* book'/'*that* book'. In each pair, the first adjective is descriptive and the second one is not, but they are all adjectives.

KEY POINT

How do you tell the difference between adjectives and adverbs?
Most adverbs add '-ly' to the adjective: 'quick'/'quickly', 'loud'/'loudly', 'happy'/'happily' (note the change from 'y' to 'i').
But beware:
- There are exceptions, especially the adverb 'well'.
- Some adjectives end in 'ly', e.g. 'ugly'.

Look at the following examples of the use of adjectives and adverbs:
'The *intelligent* (adjective) girl answered all the questions.'
'He answered *intelligently* (adverb).'
In the first case, 'intelligent' describes 'girl' (noun). She is intelligent; this is a permanent fact. In the second case 'intelligently' describes 'answered' (verb). We are only told about that one act; the boy may be wonderfully intelligent or he may just understand that one subject.

Alliteration and onomatopoeia

These are difficult words for straightforward ideas. You have probably noticed examples of alliteration and onomatopoeia in poetry without knowing the names. It is useful, though not essential, to know the correct names – and nobody will penalise you for spelling 'onomatopoeia' incorrectly!
Alliteration is the **repetition of any consonant sound**, usually at the start of a word, often enough to make an effect.
- An 'l' or 'f' sound may suggest liquid, flowing movement.
- An 's' sound may suggest softness or, sometimes, something sinister and secret.
- A 'b', 'd' or 'g' belongs with bangs, thuds and other explosive sounds – and can also suggest grandeur and power.

Continued overleaf

Remember that it is the sound, not the letter, that is important with alliteration. Reference to the 's' sound also applies to 'z', 'sh', 'ch' and, sometimes, 'c' or 'x'. Think of the difference between the 'c' sounds in 'crack' and 'cease' – if you placed these side by side, it would not be alliteration.

Onomatopoeia is the use of words that sound like their meaning: obvious examples are 'thunder', 'crash', 'boom' or 'whisper', slightly more subtle examples are 'flow', 'rivulet', 'giggle' or 'thrash'.

Answering questions

Answering questions in a timed examination is a skill in itself. You must make sure that your abilities are reflected by achieving the best possible result.

- **Read instructions carefully**. Your teacher or invigilator will probably go through them with you. It is very important to listen carefully and also to check everything for yourself.
- If there is a choice of questions, make sure that you do the number required. Writing a few lines on all the questions, instead of answering one at length, is a well-known way of losing marks in an examination.

Don't be afraid to ask your teacher or invigilator if you have any worries or difficulties. It is essential, for instance, that you know the time. Though the invigilator will rightly be annoyed if you ask the time every five minutes, generally he or she will be very willing to help.

- There are always clues on a paper. If one part of a question is worth 2 marks and another part 9 marks, you should spend much less time (and write much less) on the first one. The use of bold print should draw your attention to particularly important parts of the question and bullet points are often helpful, suggesting things you might wish to include. Pay attention to these, but add ideas of your own if you want.
- You must answer the question that has been set. In particular, be careful in Shakespeare essays to make sure you don't wander from the question into simple story-telling – it's easily done!
- Timing is important. Finishing a test ten minutes early is fine (you have time to check what you have written), but finishing 30 minutes early means you have not gone into the subject in enough depth, you have left something out or you have not developed your story at sufficient length.

- The opening and closing stages of a test are important. Use any time given at the beginning for reading and/or making notes; try to allow some (not too much) time at the end for checking your work.

SEE ALSO Notes

Apostrophes

You need to learn when not to use **apostrophes** (') as much as when to use them.
There are two reasons for using apostrophes.

Possession

An apostrophe followed by 's' shows belonging. Used at the end of a noun this shows that the next word belongs to him/her/it. For instance, 'my friend's bike', 'the teacher's briefcase', 'our team's full-back'. This is very straightforward, but there are one or two points to remember:

- We usually show plural (more than one) by adding an 's' to a noun. If you want to show plural and possession, you must place the apostrophe after the 's'. So you may be looking for 'the *boy's* football boots' (belonging to one) in 'the *boys'* changing room' (used by many boys). If you have one dog, you are 'the dog's owner'; if you have two or more, you are 'the dogs' owner'.
- If a word ends in 's' in the singular, you usually add apostrophe 's' in the usual way: 'the class's homework', 'James's sister'.
- Do not use an apostrophe when the possession word is a word in its own right: 'his', 'hers', 'theirs'. Be especially careful with 'its': 'it's' can *only* mean 'it is' or 'it has'.

Omission

When letters are left out, put an apostrophe where the letter(s) should be: 'wouldn't', 'we'll', 'I'd', etc. Make sure you put it in the right place, not necessarily between the words: 'didn't', not 'did'nt'.

Avoid using apostrophe 's' to show plural. You may see shopkeepers advertising 'HOLIDAY'S', 'APPLE'S' or 'FLOWER'S' – but that doesn't make it correct!

KEY POINT

Autobiography

A **biography** is the story of someone's life: the word means writing about life. If you add 'auto', that means 'self' (something 'automatic' works by itself), so an **autobiography** is the story of someone's life written by him or herself. You are rather young to write your autobiography, but you are frequently asked to do pieces of autobiographical writing, from variations on 'What I Did in My Holidays' to considered pieces on 'My Family' or 'Going to School'.

The key to good autobiographical writing is to mix successfully writing about events and writing about yourself. You must choose events that are interesting, then arrange them in a way that brings out that interest. Often you will choose chronological order (the order in which they happened), but you can alter it if you prefer. If you stick to chronological order, beware of two things:

- The 'Then I...' way of writing, where you keep repeating yourself.
- The feeling that you have to write equally about everything – this can be very boring; just because the first time you went fishing was interesting, it does not mean that the second and third times were as well.

Your style of writing should also create interest. Draw our attention to the parts that are exciting and amusing ('However, the most ridiculous thing my sister did happened when she first went to school.') and don't be afraid to make up dialogue (speech or conversation). Stories need dialogue and nobody expects you to remember word for word conversations that took place years ago, so write the sort of dialogue the characters would probably have used.

This is your story and a picture of yourself should emerge. If we know that you were an accident-prone little boy, we can see what's coming and that adds to the amusement.

More seriously, you might show how you became less aggressive after one or two unpleasant incidents or reveal how a year in a certain class was an ordeal for you. This is done not by writing 'I was very unhappy' several times, but by bringing it out through the events you choose to relate.

KEY POINT

It is often helpful to let your changed opinion as a mature 14-year-old show through: 'Looking back, I cannot believe how often I...' or 'I realise now that Mrs Snowden was just worried and over-worked, but at the time...'.

Blank verse

Though he is by no means the only writer to use this form, you will come across blank verse in the plays of Shakespeare. **Blank verse** is verse that **does not rhyme**, but has a **regular line length and rhythm**: ten syllables, with the stress falling on every second one.

Shakespeare uses blank verse quite freely. One of the plays you might study is *Richard III*. The famous opening lines, spoken by the Duke of Gloucester, later King Richard III, are:

'Now is the winter of our discontent
 Made glorious summer by this sun of York;'

The second line actually has eleven syllables, but the most interesting variation comes in the first line – in the first word, in fact. The stress is normally on the second syllable. Here it falls strongly on the first so that the play begins on a note of dramatic introduction: 'Now'. You will find many small variations (and some large ones) in Shakespeare's blank verse.

Not all characters speak in blank verse. Shakespeare uses it for noble characters (not the same as good characters) speaking seriously.

SEE ALSO Shakespeare, William (1564–1616), Shakespeare: key scenes

Capital letters

Use capital letters in these situations:
- When you begin a sentence.
- For all proper nouns – that is to say, the names of individual people, titles, places, buildings, etc. For example, Harry Potter, Tony Blair, Head of Lower School, Lord Mayor, Australia, Blackpool, Wembley Stadium.
- When you replace a name with its initial letter (first letter). For example, Mrs J Scott, RAC (Royal Automobile Club), WI (Women's Institute), HRH (His/Her Royal Highness).

KEY POINT

You are probably now used to websites and e-mail addresses that do not use capital letters in an ordinary way. There are very good reasons for this, but don't let it spread into the rest of your writing.

Do not use capital letters:
- in the middle of words (although pop groups and companies often do this to try to make an impact, in normal writing it is as bad as using '4' when you should write 'four')

Continued overleaf

5

- in the middle of a shortened single word: 'Ltd' (short for 'limited'), not 'L.T.D.' – that would be short for three words, 'London Trade Depot', perhaps.

SEE ALSO Sentences

Characterisation

In your SATs questions, you will probably be asked about **characterisation**, which simply means writing about what sort of person a character is. You might be asked to explain what we learn about a Shakespeare character in a certain scene or several scenes and how that fits in with the rest of the play.

- You must remember that 'character' deals with such things as honesty, intelligence, courage, responsibility, good sense, humour and so forth, not what a person looks like or how old he or she is. You could write about Richard III, 'He is a hunchback and younger brother to King Edward IV', but that is just a starting point for writing about his ruthlessness, cruelty, ambition, powers of persuasion, twisted humour, and so on.
- Some characters are straightforward. It is easy to show that Miranda in *The Tempest* is pure and innocent ('and prompt me, plain and holy innocence!') or that Dogberry in *Much Ado About Nothing* is foolish, vain and comical ('O that he were here to write me down an ass!'). Simply explain the character point, give useful examples, then use suitable quotations as evidence.
- Be prepared to discuss characters that are less straightforward. Prospero, for instance, seems good and other-worldly, but how do you account for his treatment of Caliban and, to some extent, Ariel? Richard III is evil, certainly, but does he have any redeeming features or any excuse?

EXAM TIP

In your SATs, you have time to plan an essay and make notes. Make sure that you use it well. You must avoid changing your mind during an essay. An example of a poor essay would be one that begins by saying that Prospero is good and kind, tells part of the story of the play and then writes about him as cruel. This is very different from an essay that explains the variety of behaviour we see in Prospero during the play.

SEE ALSO Shakespeare: characters

Clauses and phrases

Each sentence consists of at least one clause. Although you are not asked questions on clauses as such, it is very helpful to learn what a clause is: it is the only sure way to write in proper sentences.

A clause may have many different elements in it, but it always contains two essential parts:

- A **main verb** (or finite verb). This is a word of doing or being which relates to a particular time (the tense of the verb – usually past, present or future). For instance, 'ran' is a main (finite) verb relating to the past, but 'running' is not because it could relate to any time ('I am running', 'he was running', 'she will be running').

- A **subject,** which is a noun or pronoun telling us who or what does/did the verb. The subject can be more than one word, e.g. 'Romeo and Juliet (subject) fell (verb) in love.' The only exception to this is commands (orders). A subject is not necessary because the command makes obvious who is to do the action. If the teacher says to you, 'Bring that book to me', it is clear that you will be the subject of the verb 'bring'.

Any group of words without a finite verb is a **phrase**. In written work, unless you have some good reason (conversation, poetry, etc.), you should not place a phrase on its own between full stops: a phrase is never a sentence.

Look at these two lists.

Clauses (main verbs in italic)

We *won*.
Give me that ruler.
Vicky *was* last out of the room.
The stranger *came* running up to me.

Phrases

down by the river
scoring a goal
the best result in the tests
in the cupboard next to the blackboard

You will notice that clauses are not necessarily longer than phrases. They can be just two words or, in the case of a command, one word: 'Sit!' or 'Enter!'

A piece of writing made up solely of short sentences of a single clause each would be very boring, so you should:

- build them up with interesting phrases
- look at the **Conjunctions** section in this book for ways to join clauses together.

SEE ALSO Sentences

Colons

The **colon** (:) is often under-used by young writers, but it is a very useful punctuation mark and has three specific uses in the middle of a sentence:

- To introduce a list. There is no need for a colon plus a dash, though some people prefer it:
  'I had too much homework last night: Science, French, English and Maths.'
- To explain what has just been written: 'You should not throw things around the classroom: you might hurt someone.'
- To tell us more about the first part of the sentence: 'I met my cousin for the first time last week: he's only my age, but he's nearly six feet tall.'

A colon can also be used to introduce speech:

Ruth asked: 'Could you understand the English homework?'

In that case a comma would be equally correct, but you use a colon when introducing quotations or lengthy examples, as in several examples on this page.

Comedies

You are used to comedy as a term meaning 'something to make you laugh'. So we have 'stand-up comedians' and 'situation comedies' (sit-coms). If you are studying *Much Ado About Nothing* (and, especially, if you go to see it on stage), you will, hopefully, find it funny, but the term 'Shakespearean comedy' also refers to a specific type of play:

- The events in a Shakespearean comedy have the potential to turn into tragedy. In particular, the story of Hero nearly has a tragic outcome, but there are many other characters (Don John in his plotting, Leonato the outraged father) who act and speak with serious intent. However, tragedy is avoided: the happy ending, with characters reconciled and understanding themselves better, is an important element. In *Much Ado About Nothing* the last words are of Don John's arrest, but the play ends with a dance. The villain will be punished, but all other quarrels (Beatrice with Benedick and Don Pedro and Claudio with Leonato's family) end in reconciliation and marriage.
- The plots (story-lines) are very complicated, based on misunderstandings and deception.
- There is no single main character. Richard III is clearly the leading character in the play of that title. However, in *Much Ado About Nothing*, Beatrice and Benedick are probably the leading characters, but the main plot line concerns the romance of Claudio and Hero, and there are many other significant characters, from the highest (Don Pedro) to the lowest (the Watch).

- The settings are timeless and distinctly un-English, though working class characters tend to be very English. *Much Ado About Nothing* is set in Italy, most of the characters have Italian names, but the chief working class character is called Dogberry!
- Types of comedy vary from sophisticated aristocratic word-play (e.g. Beatrice and Benedick) to cheerfully vulgar merriment (e.g. the Watch). Several of Shakespeare's comedies, though not *Much Ado About Nothing*, include a jester.

Much Ado About Nothing is a comedy in the sense explained above, but you can also use comedy in the sense of 'something that amuses': 'The comedy increases with the deception of Benedick' or, when writing about *Richard III*, 'Richard's appearance between the bishops brings in an element of black comedy.'

EXAM TIP

SEE ALSO Shakespeare, William (1564–1616), Shakespeare: characters

Commas

The **comma** (,) is without doubt the most over-used punctuation mark. In particular, too many people let their work flow on with no full stops, but also no **conjunctions** (joining words). To use the comma correctly, your first task is to be clear about what a sentence is: you do not place a comma at the end of a sentence. Secondly, you need to know the uses of colons and semi-colons: there are situations when it is better to use one of these than a comma.

The reasons for the difficulties with the comma are that it has so many uses and some of them are optional. Read these three sentences:

'I turned to leave the room, and Kerry immediately shouted at me.'

'We brought the wood, the tools, our lunch-box, and a flask of tea.'

'When he saw me, he looked up.'

Most people would leave out the first two underlined commas and put in the third, but your teacher is unlikely to mark any of them wrong, whether you include or omit the commas. Part of the function of a comma is simply to mark out different stages of a sentence and the correct use is the one that makes that clear.

Commas are used in such situations as:
- after the words in a list (usually not the last one before 'and')
- separating clauses in a sentence
- introducing speech (though some people prefer a colon)
- separating quoted speech from inserted phrases and clauses like 'she said'

Continued overleaf

- where the smallest of punctuation marks is needed to indicate a gap or pause.

EXAM TIP

A sure sign of rushing an examination paper is when commas appear all over the page instead of full stops. Another one is when paragraphs go on for ever. In your SATs you do not have time to spend ten minutes thinking about the next word, but you should have enough time to avoid these obvious signs of lack of organisation.

SEE ALSO Colons, Conjunctions, Full stops, Semi-colons, Sentences

Conjunctions

Conjunctions are simply joining words. Think of the word 'junction' which refers to where two or more roads, railway lines or even electric cables join together. Conjunctions join together different clauses in the same sentence. Look at these examples:
'Louise opened the door, she gave a scream, she saw a spider in the corner.'
This is wrong: there are three clauses separated only by commas.
'Louise opened the door. She gave a scream. She saw a spider in the corner.'
This is correct, but your writing will be really boring if all your sentences are like this.
'*When* Louise opened the door, she gave a scream *because* she saw a spider in the corner.'
This is better: the conjunctions have joined together three clauses in one sentence.
Some conjunctions link equal clauses. The one that is most often used is 'and', but there are others like 'but' and 'so'.

KEY POINT

This section is all about conjunctions joining sentences, but 'and' can, of course, link together anything: two nouns ('hope and glory', 'Arsenal and Liverpool'), two verbs ('divide and conquer', 'pass and move'), two adjectives ('bright and beautiful'), etc.

The most interesting conjunctions, though, are those that make a special connection between a main clause and a minor one. These conjunctions tell us how the two clauses fit together. For instance:

- connections of **time**: 'when', 'before', 'after', 'as', 'since', 'until'
- connections of **place**: 'where'
- connections of **reason**: 'because', 'as', 'since'
- connections of **possibility**: 'if', 'unless'
- connections of **contrast**: 'although', 'though'.

Using conjunctions wisely and imaginatively can help your style of writing considerably. Conjunctions can convey meaning as well as join clauses. Read the following sentence:

'I went to the cinema (conjunction) there was a horror film on.'

Now insert these conjunctions in turn and see how the meaning changes: 'when', 'although', 'because', 'if', 'whenever', 'unless'.

SEE ALSO Clauses and phrases, Sentences

Dashes and hyphens

Although they look very similar, dashes (–) and hyphens (-) have quite different purposes as punctuation marks.

A **hyphen** joins together **compound words**, i.e. words made up of two or more other words: 'red-headed', 'bad-tempered', 'half-time', etc. You can, to some extent, make up compounds for yourself using a hyphen. These hyphenated compounds form the stage between separate words and single words. Originally 'home' and 'work' had no connection; then teachers began setting 'home-work'; then the word became so common that it turned into 'homework'. 'Overbalance' is so common it is written as one word; 'over-confidence' still shows that it is two words joined together.

A **dash** marks an informal break in a sentence, often to mark a delay at moments of tension or comic anti-climax, e.g. 'He raised the gun, took careful aim – and drew back the trigger' or 'I strode onto the stage, paused dramatically, fixed my subjects with a haughty stare – and promptly forgot my lines.'

A dash can be used for a particular type of informal break, a *parenthesis* or insert into the main flow of a sentence, e.g. 'I looked around for Kirsty – she had been my best friend for three years – but could not see a friendly face.'

Brackets can also be used to mark a parenthesis; it's just a matter of taste and style.

Dialogue

Dialogue simply means 'two or more people speaking'. If you are writing something in play form, dialogue is all-important, of course, but a good use of dialogue is a great help in stories as well.

- Dialogue must sound natural and suitable for the person speaking. In particular, it is unconvincing if everyone uses the slang and phrasing of teenagers at the start of the 21st century.
- In a story, it is usually best to keep a balance between narration (story-telling), dialogue and (possibly) description. It is possible to write a story entirely in dialogue. More often, though, this leads to characters telling us what they are doing. This is not very interesting and not at all natural.
- The reader needs to be able to follow the different speakers easily. Take a new line for a new speaker and use speech marks accurately. If you do this (and if the conversation is between two people), you can leave out 'he said' or 'she replied' in many cases.

'Ruth, I'm so glad you're here,' said Becky, smiling. 'I thought you'd forgotten.'
'No, the train was late. I don't know why.'
'Probably leaves on the line.'
'In April?' laughed Ruth.

KEY POINT

Try to vary the normal words like 'said', 'shouted', 'remarked' and so on. By using words like 'cackled', 'laughed', 'grunted', 'frowned' and 'yawned', you can tell the reader that the character spoke and at the same time give information about his or her mood or tone of voice.

Remember that the way of setting out dialogue in a play script is quite different. The following is the above conversation as it would be in a play. Note the absence of speech marks and the way directions about mood and reaction are placed after the speaker's name:

Becky (smiling)	Ruth, I'm so glad you're here. I thought you'd forgotten.
Ruth	No, the train was late. I don't know why.
Becky	Probably leaves on the line.
Ruth (laughing)	In April?

SEE ALSO Inverted commas/speech marks/quotation marks

Diaries

A diary, whether factual or fictional, can be very moving, amusing, entertaining and gripping. However, it is a form of writing only suited to certain types of story and needs to be used with care.

- A diary focuses on one character, so this character must be interesting.
- The way things unfold day by day is important.
- A situation based on tension or repeated routine is very suitable for diary form.

If you write a piece in diary form:

- Always be aware of the day/date. It spoils the story to spill over into the next day or to write about things you only found out afterwards.
- Be careful with repetition. It can build tension, but can also be boring. It's all a matter of what details you repeat. Marking off days on a wall in prison could work well and, in a lighter style, so could amusing variations on morning routines.

A diary is personal to the writer. Make sure it reflects the character and views of the person writing it (who might be you or someone you've invented). It can even use codes, abbreviations, etc., but remember that there is a second audience: your teacher or whoever else reads it. This reader must be able to understand it.

KEY POINT

Diction

Diction is simply the **choice of words** a writer makes. Suggestions about your own use of appropriate diction are made in the sections on **Formal and informal** and **Register**. However, what if you are asked to comment on the diction of a piece on which you have been set questions? What terms can you use?

The simplest way to comment on diction is to ask yourself the question, 'Is there anything unusual about the choice of words in this passage?' If the answer is no, then you can describe it as 'straightforward' or 'conventional' or simply write, 'There is nothing unusual about the diction.' If you find something unusual, you must find a word to describe it. Here are some words you might find useful:

- 'Simple' – when the words are short and in common use. If they are aimed at the very young, you might describe the diction as 'childish' or 'juvenile'. If the words are so short that most have one syllable, you could use 'monosyllabic'.
- 'Technical' – when the words are associated with a particular skill or technique; everything from motor mechanics to football, from banking to the Internet.

Continued overleaf

13

- 'Complicated'– the obvious term for too many long words! If the diction is really hard to understand, it is 'obscure'.
- 'Contemporary' – really up to date. The opposite is 'archaic' (not just old, but out of date).
- 'Colloquial' – literally 'like in speech'. The opposite would probably be formal.
- 'Personal' – if the writer has a very unusual style which seems unique to him or her.

If none of these words fits what you want to say about diction, don't be afraid to use a word out of your ordinary vocabulary. If the writer seems to you to be using words in a vague, educated, trendy or repetitive way, just say so.

Dictionary

There are two main uses for a dictionary and two types of dictionary that you might use:
- You should have a small or medium-sized dictionary of your own or school issue which you have with you regularly when working (including when you are preparing for tests). In some situations a large dictionary can be too cumbersome for your purposes, but you need a sound and accurate guide to spellings and meanings.
- You need to have access to a larger volume as well, perhaps in the school library or your classroom, and ideally somewhere at home as well. This enables you to look up more obscure words which you occasionally need. If it is large enough, you can find fuller, more detailed definitions and increase your knowledge of where words come from (*etymology*).

Make sure you understand the code of abbreviations used in the dictionary. 'v.', 'n.' and 'adj.' for 'verb', 'noun' and 'adjective' would be pretty easy, but a dictionary may also include such things as 'arch.' ('archaic' – out of date), 'pl.' ('plural' – if a noun has an unusual plural) or 'colloq.' ('colloquial' – informal).

It may seem obvious, but you can use a dictionary well only if you know your alphabet thoroughly.

Remember that, in alphabetical order, if the first letter is the same, you move to the second and so on to whatever letter it takes. Read the following – they are in correct alphabetical order: rescue; residence; resident; residue; restive; restless; restoration; restore.

Drafting

Preparing your essay, story or account thoroughly before you start writing is very important.

In your actual SATs you will not have time to go through a full drafting procedure, but even here you will be able to jot down notes to help with your final version.

Remember that quantity is not the only thing. In their coursework many young people work really hard and produce good pieces of 20-plus sides each. It is often better to spend the same time producing excellent pieces of ten sides or fewer.

Professional writers take their work through many **drafts** (versions of the piece) before they regard it as finished. You would not be expected to get as far as a fifth (or fifteenth!) draft, but in your classwork and homework, drafting is a good habit to develop.

- Start with the different **points** you wish to include. Write them down in any order; draw on your imagination and/or information to think of as many good ideas as possible.
- Put them in a **logical order**: keep it as simple as possible, maybe just numbers. At this point, you are preparing for later paragraphing, though your paragraphs are unlikely to coincide exactly with your numbered points.
- **Write a version** without worrying too much about spelling and punctuation. Use abbreviations if you want.
- Take a long, hard look at your first draft: alter the order if it's confusing; liven it up or shorten it if it's boring; add details to increase sense or interest; carefully check spelling and punctuation.
- Write the **second draft**. Whether there has to be a third depends on another examination of what you have written.
- If you are using a computer, the various stages may be blurred (you can be making corrections all the time), but the principle remains the same – in fact, drafting becomes easier if you use a computer.

This is the ideal method. Sometimes, for good reason, your teacher will give you time limits or ask you to write something down straightaway. This is fine, but remember that the way to produce your best (when you have time) is by careful drafting.

SEE ALSO Notes

Exclamation marks

You can use **exclamation marks** (!) in two similar, but slightly different, situations:

- When you are using a word or phrase which is an exclamation in itself: as simple as 'Oh!' or 'Ah!' or as elaborate as 'fossilised fish-hooks!' The exclamatory words like 'Oh!' and 'Ah!' are always followed by an exclamation mark, though it may sometimes be delayed for a word or two: 'Ah, Mr Foster! Where is your class?'
- When you wish to indicate that an ordinary sentence is dramatic, surprising, aggressive or shocking. Look at the following examples:

  'Claire, your homework is missing again.' 'Claire, your homework is missing again!'

  'He said he was my brother.' 'He said he was my brother!'

The exclamation marks suggest that the teacher is angry and that the second person is surprised: maybe the other boy is not telling the truth.

KEY POINT

Remember that an exclamation is a terminal point: it comes at the end of a sentence like a full stop or question mark. Normally, therefore, it should be followed by a capital letter, even when the exclamation is not a full sentence.

Fiction

Fiction is **invented narrative**: that is, a story made up by the author. You are not tested on fiction at Key Stage 3, but any good student of English will be reading fiction widely, including the latest best-sellers, but also including well-known and established novels and stories. Here are some pointers to your reading of fiction:

- The term fiction includes two different types of work: the novel and the short story. A novel is a lengthy piece of work. At least one English novel stretches to 2000 pages, but somewhere around 200 to 400 pages is very common. It is likely to have a wide range of characters and several plots. A short story tends to concentrate on one character or story-line and might be as short as three pages, though 20 to 30 is more common.
- Why not keep a reading diary? If you do, it helps greatly to write down your opinion of the book. You can do better than 'I liked it – it was fun', but even that is a useful comment. Make good use of whatever libraries are available, both in school and in your local area.
- You will be writing fiction yourself: set by your teacher and, maybe, for your own enjoyment. The more well-written fiction you read, the better your own writing will become.

First and third person

When you are writing a story, you have a choice between two forms of narrative (story-telling): first person and third person.

First person narration means that the story is told as 'I' by a character in the story. This could be yourself, but it need not be. You can invent a character and then tell the story in his or her words. This lets you reveal the thoughts and feelings of your main character. However, you must be very careful. The story-teller does not necessarily know what other characters are doing. This is good for building tension, but, if you forget and start telling the reader about things the narrator cannot know, the story becomes very unconvincing.

First person narratives might seem ideal for adventures, chases and stories of danger. They can be, but remember that dead men tell no tales. One of the feeblest (and surprisingly frequent) endings in young people's stories is, 'And then I died.'

Third person narrative means that all characters are talked about as 'he', 'she' or 'they'. The normal form is what is known as the **omniscient narrator** (the storyteller who knows all the facts). This type of narrator takes no part in the story, though he may comment on characters and events, and keeps the reader up to date on everything that is happening.

If your story is long enough and you have a good reason for doing it, you can change between first and third person – or between two or more first person narrators. But take care not to change accidentally: if your story has been all about 'Nicky', don't suddenly slide into 'I'.

SEE ALSO Narrative writing, Plot and theme

Formal and informal

In both spoken and written work, you need to be aware of the difference between formal and informal English. The word 'formality' is defined in one dictionary as 'conformity to rules' and formal English is strictly correct, done entirely by the rules. Informal English is best defined by saying what it is not: it does not worry so much about strict correctness, though that is no excuse for poor spelling, lack of clarity, etc.

Continued overleaf

In spoken English it is usual to use non-sentences and colloquial phrases ('colloquial' means 'as in speech'), even slang. This is still perfectly acceptable in classroom activities when working with partners or in groups, even in serious discussion. Your speech changes slightly when you are speaking to figures in authority: for example, the head of your school, or even your English teacher! For formal speech you need to take things a stage further. If you are presenting a report to the class or formally putting the views of your group, you need to:

- make use of correct sentence construction
- maintain politeness: this is not just a matter of not being nasty to people, but of giving them their correct names and titles, acknowledging their opinions, disagreeing without being openly rude, etc.
- prepare well enough to speak with fluency and in a logical order
- make sure that your diction is understandable to everyone.

In written work you also need to be aware of the difference between formal and informal English. Perhaps the most informal written work is in diary form, when you are writing for yourself; the most formal might be a letter to someone you need to impress (e.g. booking a school trip, applying for a job). Essays dealing with ideas or with literature should be formal in style, but stories in the first person can be much more informal.

SEE ALSO Diction, Register

Full stops

You must remember to use a **full stop** (.) at the end of every sentence – unless it is a question (?) or an exclamation (!). Be careful not to use commas at the end of sentences. For an explanation of what a sentence is, see **Sentences**.

You might think that punctuation has been set in a fixed form for some time and is not going to change. The use of the full stop shows that this is not so. Until recently a full stop was always used at the end of a word to indicate an **abbreviation** (shortened form). However, in the last few years, it has become usual to omit the full stop (for example, 'BBC' instead of 'B.B.C.'). It is impossible to say what attitude your teacher will take to this, but most people would consider both to be correct. If you prefer not to use full stops, make sure you never use them for abbreviations. If you like using them, look at the following examples and remember that a full stop for an abbreviation is only used at the end of a word:

- Mr. J. Wilcox (short for 'Mister' and 'John')
- B.B.C. (British Broadcasting Corporation)
- l.b.w. (leg before wicket)
- etc. (et cetera – Latin for 'and the rest'; note it should be 'etc.', not 'e.t.c.' – only one word is abbreviated)
- Yorks. (Yorkshire – there are some slightly odd county abbreviations, like 'Hants.' for 'Hampshire')
- Sept. (September).

Histories (history plays)

Many authors write plays that deal with an earlier period of history. You may well have seen some plays of this sort on television. However, so far as your study at Key Stage 3 is concerned, the term 'history plays' refers to ten plays by Shakespeare that present an Elizabethan view of English history.

There are two individual plays (*King John* and *Henry VIII*), but most of the plays fall into two *tetralogies* (sets of four plays):

- *Richard II; Henry IV, Part One; Henry IV, Part Two; Henry V.*
- *Henry VI, Part One; Henry VI, Part Two; Henry VI, Part Three; Richard III.*

Though the action is not always continuous, they form a sequence from play to play, often with the same characters reappearing.

If you are studying a history play, it will be *Richard III*. You should note that it comes at the end of a tetralogy and so many of the characters, including Richard, have appeared in the *Henry VI* plays. Many of the events referred to, especially early on in scenes like the wooing of Lady Anne, have already been shown on stage in the earlier plays.

However, *Richard III* is more of a stand-alone play than most of those in the tetralogies. The full title is *The Tragedy of King Richard III* and it focuses more on the central character than most of the histories. To some extent, therefore, we can look at *Richard III* as a single tragedy and there is a note about the play in the **Tragedies** section.

However, in your study, you should also be aware of its place at the end of a tetralogy of histories:

- You need to make sure you know the basic facts of the Wars of the Roses, a civil war between the Royal Houses of York and Lancaster. At the start of the play 'this sun (son) of York' (Richard's brother Edward) has just triumphed over the Lancastrian king, Henry VI.

Continued overleaf

- Richard, either before or during the play, is responsible for the deaths of many from both Royal Houses, so that the widows of Henry VI and his son appear, as well as Edward IV's wife, later widow.
- Shakespeare wrote the histories in the reign of Queen Elizabeth, a Tudor, so they present a Tudor view of history. This is particularly true of *Richard III* where Richmond, founder of the House of Tudor and Elizabeth's grandfather, is shown as an ideal hero ('Virtuous and holy, be thou conqueror!').
- Most of Shakespeare's histories show a cross-section of English life, often comically. This is less true of *Richard III*, though the people of London play a part.

SEE ALSO Shakespeare, William (1564-1616), Shakespeare: characters

Inverted commas/speech marks/ quotation marks

In your school you may use one or more of the above terms for the same thing (' 'or " "). All three terms are correct.

Speech marks are used when you are quoting somebody's exact words, either an author or a character. Remember that speech marks are used only when you quote the exact words. For example:

Mary said, 'I'm just going to the shops,' but *Mary said that she was just going to the shops.*

As speech marks are used only for the exact words, you must close and open them again around *he shouted*, *my mother remarked*, etc., if you place these within the speech:

'I'm going out,' Mary said, 'but only to the shops.' Remember also to close the speech marks at the end of any speech.

KEY POINT

If you quote an exclamation or question, make sure that the exclamation mark or question mark is inside the speech marks: 'Is that the time?', not 'Is that the time'? Full stops go inside the speech marks if the quotation is a complete sentence standing alone, but outside the speech marks if the quotation is not a whole sentence. For example:

> In the first chapter, Rav is described in detail: 'Rav was slight of build, with long, dark, wavy hair.'
> We know that Rav has 'long, dark, wavy hair'.

You can, if you wish, use inverted commas for titles of books, films, etc., though you may prefer underlining or italics: 'The Machine Gunners' or *The Machine Gunners* or The Machine Gunners.

The use of either single or double speech marks is correct: use whichever you like best, but be consistent. If you are quoting someone's words inside another speech, use the form (double or single) other than the one you are using normally. Both these examples are correct:

'Claire,' said Jo, 'I don't know what Mrs Spencer wants. She said, "Come to my room at once."'

"Claire," said Jo, "I don't know what Mrs Spencer wants. She said, 'Come to my room at once.'"

SEE ALSO Dialogue

Letters, formal

Formal letters are used in situations where you don't know the person you are writing to and where you need to be polite, for example, when you are carrying out a business transaction, sending for goods, applying for a job, etc. The layout of the letter is important, though with the coming of computers, changes have occurred. For instance, it is now normal to remove some of the punctuation: the commas and full stops in the addresses, the comma in the date and the commas after the salutations ('Dear…' and 'Yours…'). The old-fashioned version is used here to show where to put the punctuation if you want to: just make sure that you are consistent. Some other variations would also be acceptable – so long as the same information is included and the tone is suitably polite!

[Do not include your own name] 32, Windsor Close,
Poole, Dorset BH15 9JY

17th May, 2006

Mrs. J.R. Moseley,
Sunshine Travel,
Gray Street,
Bournemouth BH1 6ER

Dear Mrs. Moseley, *[It helps to know the name, otherwise 'Dear Sir' or 'Dear Madam']*

I am writing to confirm my booking of a week's holiday in Majorca for the week beginning October 21st… *[Your letter should be polite, clear, well organised and well paragraphed and contain all necessary details.]*

Yours sincerely, *[or 'Yours faithfully' if you've used 'Dear Sir' or 'Dear Madam']*

Joanne Brown *[Some people show off with unreadable signatures, but this is not a good idea. You may wish to print your name below your signature if it is not easily readable.]*

Letters, informal

You may be asked to write an account of events in the form of an informal letter for your SATs. The layout is much less important than with a formal letter, but even so you should not regard it as simply an invitation to tell a story.

- Normally, with an informal letter you should include the basic form of letter layout: address, date, 'Dear...' and some phrase to sign off. This will vary, of course, because some letters are more informal than others – writing to a schoolfriend is not the same as writing to your aunt.
- The most important thing to remember is to be aware of the audience: who is the letter for? When you are writing, think about:
  - how much the recipient of your letter knows of these events
  - whether he or she shares your opinions
  - what he or she thinks about the characters involved
  - what will entertain/amuse/surprise him or her.
- A letter will probably begin and end with personal greetings, questions, etc., but the most important thing is to tell a story or put a point of view across in an organised way. Though the letter is informal, paragraphing still matters.

EXAM TIP

In a letter it is natural to write near the beginning, 'Something amazing happened last week...' or 'I know you'll be amused to hear...'. This is also a good way of showing the examiner that you have considered your audience and how you expect him/her to respond.

SEE ALSO Formal and informal, Letters, formal

Metaphors and similes

Something that actually happened or is there in front of us is said to be literally true. However, many writers (especially poets) often use **figurative language**. This is not literally true, but it is not false or untrue either. It 'stands for' or is compared to the truth. The two main forms of figurative comparisons are **metaphors** and **similes**.

In ordinary speech, we use metaphors and similes constantly. Most of them have been used so often that they have no life in them. There is nothing to be gained by using phrases like 'as dead as a dodo', 'as good as gold' or 'coming down in buckets'. If you use metaphors and similes, you should show some originality.

Make sure you avoid the mistaken use of the word 'literally'. 'I was literally frozen to the spot' does not make sense unless the author is actually in sub-zero temperatures: it is a metaphor (a rather over-used one), not literal truth.

The difference between metaphors and similes is straightforward:
- A **simile** is an **open obvious comparison** – which means that it usually uses 'like' or 'as', though 'than' or some other word may be used occasionally.
- A **metaphor** is a **hidden implied comparison**. The statement is not literally true, but is written as though it is. If you wanted to compare a sudden burst of noise to a tidal wave, you could write, 'A tidal wave of noise engulfed him.' The same idea using a simile would read, 'The noise hit him like a tidal wave.'

You can judge the effectiveness of a simile or metaphor by:
- how appropriate it is
- how striking it is
- how memorable it is.

There is no point in using figurative language unless it makes sense: it must be appropriate. However, the most powerful metaphors and similes are much more than just appropriate.

When you are studying Shakespeare's plays you will come across many striking uses of metaphor and simile. You will be expected to show how metaphor adds to our understanding of the play: for instance, the animal metaphors ('hedgehog', 'toad') which Lady Anne uses to insult Richard of Gloucester, the multiple metaphors and similes in Prospero's speech beginning 'You do look, my son,' or the witty metaphors between Beatrice and Benedick.

SEE ALSO Personification

Narrative writing

Narrative writing is simply 'writing that tells a story'. You are familiar with the word 'narrator', which means the person who tells a story. You are likely to have to write narratives of two sorts:

- **Ordered narratives of fact** These might take the form of reports and are likely to be based on actual events or a situation that you have been given. These narratives must be clear and well-arranged. Apart from writing clearly (good arrangement of sentences, suitable diction, etc.), a key element is effective paragraphing.
- **Imaginative narratives** These will probably be stories you make up or perhaps imaginative re-tellings of events in your own life. They should still be clear and well-planned, but the plan need not be the conventional one. Try to organise your story in an imaginative and original way.

SEE ALSO Autobiography, First and third person, Plot and theme

Newspapers

You may be asked to answer questions on articles from newspapers or the newspapers themselves. Though everything in newspapers (except opinion columns) is supposed to be factually true, there are different ways of presenting truth. You should ask yourself questions about the intentions and methods of the editor of the paper:

- What effect does the layout of a newspaper page have? Traditionally broadsheets (the larger, more serious papers) have more stories, smaller headlines and smaller pictures than the tabloids (the smaller, more popular papers). In recent years several of the broadsheets have adopted a smaller format: *The Independent* and *The Times* use the term 'compact' and *The Guardian* is now of a size known as 'Berliner'. You might find it interesting to compare their front pages with a traditional broadsheet like the *Daily Telegraph*.
- What sort of reader does the editor or columnist have in mind?
- What influence does the editor or columnist wish to have? Are they starting a campaign against the England football manager? Are they persuading the reader for or against the government?
- Is the paper or the article really honest and fair?
- Has the writer managed to make news interesting? How do you tell the truth and present news fairly, yet still interest and entertain people so that they buy your paper?

Notes

The right preparation for written work is important. In your SATs you will not have the time to work through various drafts, but that does not mean that you cannot prepare your written work. Time is allowed, and space given, for making notes. The reason for making notes is so that you avoid confusion in your essay or answer.

The task of note-making consists of two main stages:

- You should write down your **ideas** in any order. Don't write in full sentences (that takes too long), use abbreviations and don't worry about handwriting. The important thing is that *you* understand the notes, not anybody else, and, if you always write 'charac' for 'character' or 'imp' for 'importance', that is sensible and understandable.
- Decide on the **order** you are going to use for your various points. Group together similar ideas – or, sometimes, opposite ideas – and make sure the essay has a shape. Then mark your notes in some way to indicate the order: use numbers, brackets, lines and circles linking different notes, etc.

EXAM TIP

It is unlikely that you will fail to finish any piece of writing in your SATs. However, if you find that time is nearly up and you haven't finished, stop writing your essay three to four minutes early and write down in note form what you were going to write if you had had another 20 minutes. These notes should be neat enough for the examiner to read, but don't use proper sentences, otherwise you might just as well carry on writing the essay.

SEE ALSO Drafting

Nouns

You are probably used to nouns being called 'naming words'. This is a perfectly good definition so long as you remember that it is not always the name of an individual ('James' or 'Blackpool'), but is more likely to be the general name of a type of thing or being ('boy' or 'town'). You should know three main types of noun:

- Common: the general name of the object, person, category, etc.
- Proper: the name belonging to an individual – always beginning with a capital letter.
- Collective: the name for a group of things, people, etc.

Look at the following examples:

Common	Proper	Collective
footballer	Wayne Rooney	team
girl	Tracy	class, club, family, etc.
dog	Spot	pack

A proper noun can involve more than one word, e.g. 'Manchester United', 'Hillcrest High School' or 'Milton Keynes'. Every word has a capital letter, unless it is a short word deemed to be unimportant, as in 'United States of America' or 'Babes in the Wood'.

KEY POINT

Collective nouns are singular. Because there are several persons or objects involved, we tend to use plurals for them: we say, 'Our class are going to Alton Towers'. In informal situations this is perfectly acceptable, but the strictly correct version is, 'Our class *is* going to Alton Towers.'

SEE ALSO Pronouns

Paragraphs

One of your tasks when writing is to make it as easy as possible for the reader to find his or her way through and to follow the argument, point of view or story-line of your piece. This is most effectively done by intelligent and careful paragraphing.

There is no answer to the question, 'How long should a paragraph be?' except, perhaps, 'as long as it needs to be'. However, you should not let a paragraph stretch to a second side or make all your paragraphs one sentence long, unless you have a very good reason for doing so.

You can obtain good effects by varying length. After a lengthy, dramatic and descriptive paragraph, think of the effect of a short four or five word paragraph: 'Trembling, she looked down.' or 'They were no longer alone.'

Each paragraph should be about something. If you are reporting on a situation or writing about a Shakespeare play, for instance, the reader should be able to follow the main points of the essay through paragraph by paragraph. In an essay, it helps very much to start each paragraph with a topic sentence to tell the reader what it is about – and to keep you on the subject:

- 'In this scene it is obvious that Beatrice and Benedick are mocking each other.'
- 'This passage deals with the reasons why holidays abroad have increased.'

- 'If I had to plan a night's viewing on television, my priority would be to make it as varied as possible.'

You can spend the rest of the paragraph going into more detail about the topic being covered.

In a story, your organisation should suit your own plans, but even here the openings of paragraphs can help point the way through the story:

- 'Meanwhile, the search party was still scrambling up the rock face.'
- 'Now it was quite clear to Tom that he had only one option left.'
- 'As the evening wore on, I had less and less idea what I would do if the phone rang again.'

Parts of speech

The term 'parts of speech' refers to the jobs which words do: some words are the names of things, some join up statements, some express action, etc. Your study of English will be made easier if you know the seven main parts of speech: **noun, verb, adjective, adverb, pronoun, preposition** and **conjunction**. There are sections in this book explaining the functions and forms of all seven.

Though you do not specifically have to answer questions on parts of speech, you need to be confident in understanding and using these terms. For example, if you wish to explain how an author creates a frightening mood, you might mention that he or she is using many eerie and menacing adjectives.

Personification

Personification is a special form of metaphor. With personification an inanimate object (that is, one without animal life) is given human form. Many countries have national personifications: Britain becomes Britannia, the United States has Uncle Sam. More often, a poet uses personification rather more subtly. The poet John Keats wrote:

'Those green-rob'd senators of mighty woods,
Tall oaks...'

He is comparing oaks to senators without using 'like' or 'as': that is a metaphor. However, he is also comparing trees to people: senators are members of a ruling chamber (senate) and Keats is probably thinking of Ancient Rome. So the leaves and foliage of the trees become the robes of the senators. Keats has written of things as though they are people: personification.

SEE ALSO Metaphors and similes

Plot and theme

Plot and theme are different ways to explain what a play or story is about. If you were asked, 'What is *Richard III* about?', you could answer in two ways:

- 'It's about Richard, Duke of Gloucester who has helped his brother to fight his way to the throne as Edward IV. When his brother dies, Richard, with the assistance of the Duke of Buckingham, kills or subdues all rivals and opponents, including his nephews, and seizes power. Eventually King Richard is overthrown by Henry of Richmond.'
- 'It's about ambition and the nature of evil. It deals with issues of kinship, right and responsibility and examines physical and moral deformity.'

Both are correct answers to the question. The first deals with the plot; the second deals with themes.

In writing about Shakespeare, you are most likely to have to deal with plot and characterisation, but an awareness of themes is very helpful.

You should also be aware of the importance of handling the plot well in your own stories. Thinking up a good story is important, but so is presenting that story effectively. The two essentials are:

- to make the story convincing
- to make it interesting/amusing/exciting/dramatic.

Prefixes

A prefix is a syllable or several syllables **with a regular set meaning** added to the beginning of a word. The most useful thing about prefixes is that you can work out the meaning of a new word for yourself. Let us take a word with two prefixes: 'antepenultimate'.

- First of all, you need to know the meaning of 'ultimate'. It means 'last', as in 'the ultimate sanction'.
- Then you take the prefix 'pen' which means 'almost', as in 'peninsula' – 'almost an island'. So 'penultimate' means 'almost last' – 'last but one'.
- Then you add 'ante' which means 'before' as in 'anteroom' (a room before the main one) or 'ante meridiem' (a.m. – before noon). Thus we end up with 'before almost last' – 'last but two'.

You can even use prefixes to make up new words. Many new words have been created in recent years using 'trans' (across), 'mega' (great or huge), 'super' (over or beyond), 'hyper' (over or excessive) or 'multi' (many). Markets have existed for centuries, so, when a new type of shop was created, they simply added 'super' to make 'supermarkets' (more than markets) and, when even bigger ones came along, 'hyper' was pressed into service for 'hypermarkets'. The following list is useful, but it is far from complete:

anti-	against	in-	not (can also take the forms im-, ig-, ir- and il-)
auto-	self		
bi-	two (also du- and duo-)	in-	in (also means 'not')
bio-	life	inter-	between or among
co-	with or together (also con- and com-)	mono-	one
		peri-	around
demi-	half (also semi- and hemi-)	poly-	many
dis-	not	post-	after
ex-	out of or from (sometimes just e-)	pre-	before
		re-	again or in return
		sub-	below
		un-	not

SEE ALSO Reading for understanding, Suffixes

Prepositions

A preposition means 'something placed before' and that is just what it is: a preposition goes in front of a noun or pronoun to link it to the words around. Many prepositions are among the shortest words in the language: 'in', 'on', 'by', 'to', 'of', 'up', though the words that follow are also prepositions: 'near', 'below', 'beside', 'through', 'between', 'underneath'. Although some of them are short, they are very important words: use one wrongly and you confuse the whole meaning of the sentence. To understand how important the precise use of prepositions is, read the following:

'Would you get the exercise books, please? They are (preposition) the cupboard.'

You could insert 'in', 'on', 'near' or 'beside', to give very different meanings to the sentence. The word 'opposite' could even send you to the other side of the room!

Pronouns

Pronouns need to be considered along with nouns. They do exactly the same job, but are not always as specific: for instance, 'it' or 'that' could be used instead of 'the book' in the sentence 'Pass me the book.'

A pronoun takes the place of a noun. It would obviously be boring and clumsy to keep referring to 'the teacher' or 'my sister Mary' every time in a piece of writing about one person, so you use 'him' or 'her' instead. These are known as **personal pronouns**, which also include the first and second person pronouns ('I', 'you', etc.). Nouns are automatically in the third person. The full list of personal pronouns is:

First person	I	me	we	us
Second person	you	you	you	you
Third person	he	she	it	they
	him	her	it	them

A pronoun is any word replacing a noun, as in the following examples:

'I lost that ring last week.' – 'that' is not a pronoun but an adjective, because the noun 'ring' is still there.

'I lost that last week.' – now 'that' has become a pronoun – it has replaced 'ring'.

KEY POINT

If you are writing about several people, you need to be careful in your use of personal pronouns. Too many uses of 'he' and 'him' can confuse, so go back to the noun ('Jamie' or 'the man wearing dark glasses') every so often to make things clear. It is also good style to use the noun rather than the personal pronoun when beginning a new paragraph.

SEE ALSO Nouns

Prose

'Prose' is a word you may not know and you may therefore be confused by its use, including in this book. It has, however, a very simple meaning: **prose is ordinary writing or speech**. This paragraph is prose; so is your history essay. In terms of literature study, it is, quite simply, not poetry.

You will come across the word prose in your study of Shakespeare: a section in verse will be followed by a section in prose or your teacher will point out that a character usually speaks in verse, but in a certain scene uses prose. You will find generally that Shakespeare uses verse for serious, noble and formal speech and prose for informal speech, comedy and the speech of the lower classes. You might also come across the word prose in 'an anthology of poetry and prose' (a book that collects together different types of writing by different people) or the instruction to write something in 'modern prose' (ordinary writing). Your teacher may even refer to a writer's 'prose style' (the way in which he or she writes).

Question marks

The question mark (?) is, of course, used at the end of every question. This is very simple, but there are a few points to note:

- Some sentences hint at a question, but do not put it in question form: 'I wonder if the train will be on time.' This is a statement: it states that you are wondering. Therefore you use a full stop, not a question mark. However, in dialogue, you can sometimes end a sentence in statement form with a question mark. You might say, 'Have you left your mobile phone at home?' as a question, but, if you think the answer will be yes, you can say, 'You've left your mobile phone at home?'. Ordinary dialogue is less formal than writing and, in your stories or plays, this is the one situation where you can follow an apparent statement with a question mark.
- You use the question mark at the end of the sentence, not after the questioning word. 'Why? should I go to the shops' is totally wrong.
- Finish the question with a question mark before you go on to another

statement. 'Why should I go to the shops, Lindsey's doing nothing?' is wrong. The correct version is: 'Why should I go to the shops? Lindsey's doing nothing.'

If you are writing dialogue or using a quotation, the question mark comes inside the speech marks if the question is part of the speech:

Sharon said, 'Have you done your homework?'

Did he really say, 'I'm not going to my English lesson'?
In the second example, the question is in the main sentence, not in the speech.

Quotations

When you are writing about Shakespeare in your SATs, it is useful to use quotations from the play to illustrate or prove your point. Remember the following points about quotations:

- Quotations must not take over the whole essay. The quotations must not be too long (two to three lines is fine; so is two to three words) and you should not use a quotation every few lines of your essay.
- The quotation must be relevant to what you are writing. The fact that you are writing about Richard III and the quotation is about him is not enough: the quotation must support your point.
- The normal way to use a quotation is as follows.
  1   Make a point: for example, Dogberry is officious and stupid.
  2   Explain and expand: for example, you might mention the way in which he garbles and misunderstands words.
  3   Bring in a suitable quotation: for example, 'Dost thou not suspect my place?'
- Set quotations out properly. If you are using a few words, fit them into the sentence: Caliban, the 'freckled whelp hag-born', is treated by Prospero as less than human. For longer quotations, take a new line and, if it is verse, set it out in the same way as it appears in the play.
- Remember that the correct noun is 'quotation', though we use 'quote' in informal speech. So you 'quote' from Shakespeare, but you use 'quotations'.

SEE ALSO Shakespeare: key scenes

Reading for understanding

One of your most important activities in the SATs is reading for understanding or comprehension. You will be given unseen passages (ones you have had no chance to prepare) and will have time to read them and make notes before answering questions.

By '**understanding**' we mean two main things:

- Understanding the facts. You may be told that there are 30 farms in a certain valley and 10 on the surrounding hills where farming is more difficult. If in your answers you say there are 300 in the valley or reverse the figures for hills and valley or claim that farming is easier on the hills, you will have little chance of success. However, this sort of error is not difficult to avoid.
- Understanding the writer's intention. This is much harder.
  - Is the writer putting forward a particular opinion, perhaps that farmers need financial support?
  - Is he or she trying to create a certain mood? (Response to diction can help you here.)
  - Is the whole thing to be taken seriously or are there elements of humour?
  - Is he or she writing as an outsider or with a personal involvement?
  - Is he or she trying to appeal to a certain type of reader?

Of course there is always the possibility of simply not knowing some of the words, although the meanings of very difficult or unusual words are usually given at the bottom. Sometimes all you can do is guess, but there are two main techniques that you can try first:

- Break up the word. This is dealt with in both the **Prefix** and **Suffix** sections. You may know what one part of the word means or even what all the parts mean individually. The word may also remind you of another word you know. If you came across 'superabundant' for the first time, you could put together the prefix 'super-' (over) and the familiar word 'abundant' to give 'excessively plentiful'.
- Use the **context** when you have only a hint as to the meaning of a word. Instead of panicking or giving up, work out what meaning would make sense at that point. You will sometimes be wrong, but it's worth trying.

SEE ALSO Answering questions

Register

Though this use of the word may be new to you, you always need to be aware of register in your writing. What it means is the form of language you use. This has to reflect what you want to write, but also the situation of the piece of writing, whom you are writing it for, etc. Often it is a matter of making sure you use a suitably formal register, but it is possible to use a register that is too formal, too modern, too old-fashioned or simply unsuitable. Read the following three examples and note the failures of register:

'When Claudio and Don Pedro reject and accuse Hero, Leonato loses control of his grief and *goes barmy*.'

'The chairman outlined the current fiscal policy, explaining that the economic situation had brought about a cash flow problem and stressing the danger of *going broke*.'

'Try to get the ball wide. They're solid enough down the middle, but we'll have a chance if we keep play *adjacent to the perimeter*.'

The faults here are fairly obvious. In the first case, the language used is correct and formal, but suddenly a slang phrase bursts in. In the second case, it's not the lurch from formality to slang that is the problem, but the change from technical business language to the way ordinary people refer to money. In the third case, informal colloquial style suddenly turns into a geometry lesson.

KEY POINT

You will probably find it interesting to try to work out what register a newspaper or magazine is adopting. For instance, it might try to involve the reader one-to-one (personal or intimate) or use many specific terms about politics, crime, fashion or sport (technical) or try to stir up the reader's feelings (emotional).

SEE ALSO Diction, Formal and informal

Revision

For your Key Stage 3 SATs, revision is not such a major matter as it will be for GCSE and any further examinations you do. However, in the sense of 'preparing for an examination' rather than 'learning a mass of facts', it should be taken seriously.

- The most important thing you have to prepare for SATs is yourself. Make sure you know exactly what is involved in each paper. Your teacher will probably make it very clear, but, if you have any doubts, ask him or her well in advance. Get the timing firmly in your mind before the test: when the invigilator tells you how long there is for every part, it should be just a reminder. Make sure that you have a back-up for everything: two blue or black pens or biros, a watch in case you can't see the clock in the room, etc. You will be so well organised you won't need to panic!

- The second thing that needs to be at its best is your actual writing ability. This again depends on familiarity with the sorts of writing that there will be on each paper. Your teacher will have given you practice and will, no doubt, have written comments on the bottom of your work: read these, follow the advice and, if you don't understand it, ask! Keep a spelling book of essential words you are not sure of during the year and re-learn the spellings in advance of the test.
- For the Shakespeare paper, make sure that you revise the whole text, not just the key scenes. Obviously, you will spend most time on the key scenes, but you need to know how they fit in with the rest of the play. As well as the text, go back to notes and worksheets you have been given and possibly essays you have written. Don't leave Shakespeare revision until the night before the test; in fact, do as little revision as possible at the last minute.

Romances (late comedies)

Shakespeare's plays are divided into **tragedies**, **comedies** and **histories**. However, there are some that it is difficult to fit into any of these categories. Several of these plays are known as 'problem plays', mainly because they deal with a moral problem, but also, perhaps, because they are something of a problem themselves.

Several plays that Shakespeare wrote late in his career stand alone, though *The Winter's Tale* and *The Tempest*, the two best-known, are traditionally termed 'comedies'. These plays have also been called the **romances** because they deal with unreal and dream-like events.

In *The Winter's Tale* the first half of the play is like a tragedy, set in a royal court, then, after comical and romantic episodes with shepherds, the tragic story is given a happy ending by almost magical means. In *The Tempest* the tragedy is in the past (Shakespeare could have given it the title *The Tragedy of Prospero, Duke of Milan*) and all is solved by means of magic.

The Tempest is called a 'comedy' because the plot works out happily and,

Continued overleaf

35

though Prospero is the main character, attention is shared by others: the most interesting character developments can be found elsewhere. However, it is definitely not a typical Shakespearean comedy like *Much Ado About Nothing*.

Semi-colons

The semi-colon (;) is an interesting punctuation mark – one that you can avoid using altogether, but one that can give your writing more precision. Think of a semi-colon as being halfway between a comma and a full stop and use it when a comma seems too little and a full stop seems too much.

The ways in which writers use semi-colons fall into two types:

- If you are starting a new clause and there is no joining word to the rest of the sentence, you start a new sentence. However, sometimes you may think that the two sentences are so closely linked that they ought to be one. That is the job of the semi-colon:
  'On the mountain top it was bright and sunny. Down below in the valley the mist hung over the small town.'
  You can add the conjunction 'although' and use a comma: 'Although on the mountain top it was bright and sunny, down below in the valley the mist hung over the small town.'
  Alternatively, you can simply place a semi-colon in the middle: 'On the mountain top it was bright and sunny; down below in the valley the mist hung over the small town.'

- The second use is less common. It is to use the semi-colon as an overgrown comma rather than a lesser full stop. Sometimes, when you are writing a list, the various items become so long and complicated that using only commas would confuse the reader:
  'On the expedition with us were Professor Sykes, whose knowledge of the history of Peru was second to none; his wife, who always acted as his scientific assistant; Major Johnson, Captain Purdy and Sergeant Bryson of the Royal Engineers; a local guide, with his team of dogs; and, most important of all, our cook with two months' supplies.'

KEY POINT

The use of the semi-colon is often simply a matter of taste. In the first example, a full stop would also be correct, but many writers would prefer to use a semi-colon.

Sentences

A simple sentence consists of a single clause: in other words, it can be as little as subject and main verb. The subject tells you who or what did something; the main verb tells what he/she/it/they did and when. Alternatively, the clause can tell you something about what the subject is, not does.

Sentences take four main forms:

- **Statement**: 'The party (subject) finished (verb) late.'
- **Question**: 'Did (verb) you (subject) enjoy (verb) it?' (The verb is often split in two in a question; in a statement we would simply put 'enjoyed'.)
- **Exclamation**: 'What a great time we (subject) had (verb)!'
- **Command**: 'Never go (verb) to another party there.' (Commands usually don't have a subject; it's obvious that the person being spoken to is to is be the subject of the verb.)

Complex sentences are formed by joining together clauses with conjunctions to give a more varied writing style, mixing together simple and complex sentences.

SEE ALSO Clauses and phrases, Conjunctions

Shakespeare, William (1564–1616)

You have to study a play by Shakespeare for your Key Stage 3 SATs and another one for GCSE at the end of Key Stage 4. Therefore knowledge of Shakespeare is essential.

- Shakespeare wrote over 30 plays between (approximately) 1590 and 1612, in the reigns of Queen Elizabeth I and King James I.
- The plays are normally divided into three groups: comedies, histories and tragedies.
- Most of the plays were written for afternoon performance in an open-air theatre with a stage projecting into the audience. You can see a reconstruction of Shakespeare's theatre at the Globe on London's South Bank, either by going to a play or just visiting the theatre. Think how this staging would limit special effects.
- Shakespeare's plays use a mixture of prose (ordinary speech) and blank verse, particularly associated with noble characters and serious scenes.
- Questions on Shakespeare in your SATs will expect you to show understanding of character and theme as well as the events in the play.

Continued overleaf

Try not to forget that Shakespeare's plays belong in the theatre, not in the classroom. Clearly it is right to study his plays, but, if at all possible, see them on stage or film as well – it will help you understand the plays, but, most important, it will show you that Shakespeare's plays can be funny, dramatic, moving, exciting – and surprisingly easy to follow!

SEE ALSO   Blank verse, Comedies, Histories, Shakespeare: characters, Romances (late comedies), Tragedies

Shakespeare: characters

Shakespeare's plays are divided into comedies, histories and tragedies. Each of these tends to use a different set of characters.

- *Much Ado About Nothing* is a comedy. Shakespeare often used existing stories, many of Italian origin. You will find, typically, that noble characters have Italian names and lower class or rougher characters are English. In *Much Ado About Nothing* it is true that Benedick sounds faintly English, but Beatrice was seen as an Italian name and Claudio, Leonato, Hero, Don Pedro and so on are definitely Italian – or, at least, Mediterranean – and Dogberry is comically English. The witty young nobles and clownish commoners are typical, though there is no jester as in many of Shakespeare's comedies.

In writing about characters in comedy, accept the unlikely plots as 'real'. There is no point in writing, 'Don Pedro and Claudio must be really stupid to be taken in by the deception.' They are not 'really stupid', but they are selfish, over-confident and arrogant and they learn from their mistake.

- *Richard III* is a history play. Events in the history plays took place in England between the 13th and 16th centuries: in *Richard III's* case, in the late 15th century. In many of the history plays there are vivid characters invented by Shakespeare (for example, Falstaff in the *Henry IV* plays), but in *Richard III* the most interesting feature is the way in which historical characters are made to fit the Tudor view of events: the Tudor Henry of Richmond saves the country from the evil child-killer Richard.

Remember that Shakespeare was writing comparatively soon after the events. Henry VII, who succeeded Richard, was only two generations away from Elizabeth who was Queen when Shakespeare wrote the play.

- There is currently no tragedy set for Key Stage 3 SATs. However, the characters used in *The Tempest* are in many ways similar to those in tragedies. Tragedies are usually set in the distant past (*The Tempest* is set in a sort of remote no-time) in a variety of foreign lands: *King Lear*, *Cymbeline* and *Macbeth* take place in the British Isles, but none of them in a country called 'England'. Thus the foreign-sounding (in this case, Italian) kings, lords and dukes in *The Tempest* are thoroughly typical, and clownish servants also occur in several tragedies, but the treatment of supernatural and subhuman beings like Ariel and Caliban as real humans belongs only to the surreal world of *The Tempest*.

SEE ALSO Characterisation, Comedies, Histories (history plays), Romances (late comedies), Tragedies

Shakespeare: key scenes

For your SATs you have to study a Shakespeare play, but your answer in the final test is based solely on one important scene or group of scenes. You obviously are expected to know these scenes in detail. You should be familiar with:
- the events of the scene(s)
- what they show about the characters
- relationships between characters
- important images
- dramatic effect – how the scene(s) work(s) on stage.

You must also show why the scene is important to the play. As well as knowing a great deal about a character's behaviour in this scene, you need to be able to compare it to his or her actions elsewhere in the play: is this scene a turning point for the character? As well as identifying images, you need to link them to the whole play: does the imagery express a main theme?

Continued overleaf

Always remember when writing about literature that you must know the story perfectly, but are rarely asked to re-tell it. If you are asked to describe the qualities Richard III shows in a certain scene, you are not expected to go through everything he does. Use events in the play to prove your point; don't re-tell the story.

Singular and plural

Singular is the form of a noun or verb we use for one person or object; **plural** is what we use for two or more. Generally this is simple: for a noun we add 's' (without apostrophe) for the plural, for a third person verb in the present tense we remove 's'. In both cases we use 'es' following an 's' sound (or 'x', 'sh, 'ch', etc.):

Singular: 'The train approaches.'
Plural: 'The trains approach.'

It is important to make sure that agreement is always perfect: that is, that all parts of a phrase or clause fit together by using the same form, singular or plural. The verb 'to be' behaves very oddly ('is'/'are', 'was'/'were') and many common errors with agreement involve 'to be'. Avoid 'he were' and 'we was' in written work and formal oral work.

Many nouns have irregular plurals. Here are some of the main types:

- Sometimes there is no change (this is common among animals): 'cattle', 'sheep', 'deer', 'grouse'.
- Some nouns change the vowel in the middle: 'goose'/'geese', 'mouse'/'mice', 'foot'/'feet', 'man'/'men', 'woman'/'women'.
- Nouns ending in 'y' after a consonant move to 'ies' in the plural: 'factory'/'factories', 'country'/'countries'. Note that this does not apply after a vowel. 'Story' (a tale or narrative) becomes 'stories', but 'storey' (floor of a building) becomes 'storeys'.
- Nouns ending in 'f' or 'fe' often become '-ves' in the plural. This is difficult because there is no rule to show you which end in '-fs' ('chief'/'chiefs') and which in '-ves' ('half'/'halves'). The best way is to think how you would say them. In some cases ('roof'/'roofs'/'rooves', 'scarf'/'scarfs'/'scarves') both are correct.
- 'Tomatoes' and 'potatoes' add an extra 'e', but this is not the rule for all nouns ending in 'o'.
- 'Children', of course, is an unusual plural and there are one or two other old-fashioned '-en' plurals, like 'oxen'.

Remember that collective nouns are singular: 'My family goes (not 'go') back 200 years in this village.' 'Each', 'every,' 'either' and 'neither' are also singular: 'Everyone is looking forward to the SATs.'

Soliloquy

You need to know the term 'soliloquy' for your study of Shakespeare. The word literally means 'alone-speak' and that is exactly what it is. A character alone on stage expresses his or her thoughts, fears, hopes, intentions and innermost secrets to the audience. A soliloquy is a sort of 'thinking aloud' for characters on stage and, as such, characters speak the truth in soliloquies. This is a great help in understanding their true characters.

- *Richard III* makes great use of soliloquies for the very good reason that Richard of Gloucester is a great deceiver and the audience can enjoy and understand his deception much better if occasionally let inside his mind. Richard is even given a soliloquy of some 40 lines to start the play, a magnificent opening that employs all the special qualities of a soliloquy. To begin with we have a little history, then some social commentary, before he moves on to being a misfit and plotter, finishing with a specific threat against Clarence. In the next scene his sardonic sense of humour enlivens another great soliloquy, 'Was ever woman in this humour woo'd?'
- *Much Ado About Nothing* makes less use of soliloquies. Characters usually have friends, family or fellow plotters to confide in, but you should notice that, when a character is cut off from his/her friends, he/she turns to soliloquy to explain his/her feelings and attitude. The scenes in Acts 2 and 3 when Beatrice and Benedick are deceived by their friends both end with a soliloquy by the victim: Benedick even gets the chance to explain his views on love at the start of the scene.
- You may be surprised at the limited use of soliloquy in *The Tempest*. It is, after all, a play about appearance and reality and confiding in the audience might seem a part of that. For the most part, though, Prospero is demonstrating his power to others and wielding it on behalf of others. So, for instance, what might have been a soliloquy on the shipwreck and his own past becomes a lesson to Miranda.

Continued overleaf

Similar to a soliloquy is a monologue, literally 'one speak'. A monologue can be spoken by a character on his or her own, as in Alan Bennett's *Talking Heads* on television, but it does not have to be, nor is it necessarily a matter of 'thinking aloud'. Perhaps, if your class is failing to join in a discussion, your teacher might say, 'Don't turn this into a monologue!'

SEE ALSO Shakespeare: characters

Spelling

English spelling is very inconsistent. After all, the word 'though' rhymes with 'go', 'sew', snow' and 'beau', but not with 'through', 'thought' or 'trough' – and those three don't rhyme with each other either! So people say that there are no rules. This is not so, but many of the rules are often broken and many words have irregular spelling.

Although there are some spelling rules that are helpful, there are always many words that have to be learned individually. Keep a spelling book and write in it all those words you need, but didn't know until a dictionary or teacher came to your aid.

Here are some of the more helpful rules of English spelling:
- **'i' before 'e' except after 'c'** works very well as long as you add 'when the sound is "ee"'. Examples of 'e' before 'i' include 'ceiling' (after 'c'), 'either' (the sound is 'eye') and 'feign' (the sound is 'ay'). 'Their' is often mis-spelt, but here again the sound is not 'ee'. Exceptions: 'weird' and 'seize'.
- **Long and short vowels.** Long vowel sounds are 'ay', 'ee', 'eye', 'oh' and 'oo'. You can make a vowel long in many ways ('e' on the end is common), but a particularly useful rule is that the vowel before a single consonant in the middle of a word is long, before a double consonant is short. You might be 'taping' a CD or radio show or 'tapping' on the wall to attract attention.
- **'ful' endings.** These have a single 'l' ending: 'beautiful', 'cheerful', etc., though of course they double the consonant as adverbs: 'beautifully', 'cheerfully'.
- **adding 'ing'.** If the verb ends in 'e', remove it: 'waste'/'wasting', 'force'/'forcing', though we usually use 'singeing' (meaning burning) to avoid confusion with the musical 'singing'. If a single-syllable verb ends in a consonant, double it: 'run'/'running', 'hit'/'hitting'.

There are also many pairs or groups of words that are often confused. These need to be learned individually. A few common examples are:

- their (belonging to them), there (opposite of 'here'), they're (they are)
- your (belonging to you), you're (you are)
- its (belonging to it), it's (it is or it has)
- accept (receive or take), except (with the exception of 'All except…')
- passed (went by something), past (time gone by)
- principle (a rule), principal (first or chief).

You can find many more for yourself and write them in your spelling book.

Suffixes

A suffix is a syllable or syllables **with a set function** added to the end of a word. In this respect it is very like a prefix, though in a different place. A word like 'irresistible' has a main word-stem, 'resist', in the middle, with a prefix and suffix altering its meaning. 'Ir-' is one of the negative prefixes (a version of 'in-' which is used before 'r') and 'ible' means 'able'. Therefore 'ir-resist-ible' means 'not able to be resisted'.

Suffixes in general affect meaning less than prefixes. Many simply change the part of speech.

For example, you will find many suffixes forming abstract nouns (ones dealing with ideas, states and feelings, not persons or things): '-ness' ('happiness'), '-dom' ('wisdom') and '-hood' ('manhood').

Sometimes suffixes do affect the meaning as well as the part of speech:

- Add '-ful' and '-less' to words like 'help' and 'fear' and you get opposite meanings.
- The suffixes '-ible' and '-able' both mean 'able'. Unfortunately, there is no rule as to which one is used. You simply have to remember that 'able to be laughed at' is 'laughable' and 'able to be seen' is 'visible'.

SEE ALSO Prefixes

43

Tragedies

Many of Shakespeare's plays come into the category of tragedies. Tragedies are not just plays in which terrible things happen to people. They have certain qualities that make them quite different from other Shakespearean plays. At present no tragedy is set for Key Stage 3 SATs, but *Richard III* is one of two of Shakespeare's history plays to be described in the title as a tragedy. If that is the play you are studying, you might wish to read the following comments on the nature of Shakespeare's tragedy and decide how many are true of *Richard III*.

- The setting is always remote in time or place or both. Though they are set in 'real' places (Ancient Britain, Denmark, Scotland, etc.), the stories are not historically true. The Roman tragedies such as *Julius Caesar* probably have most historical content.
- All feature one **protagonist** (central character) except for the three love tragedies: *Romeo and Juliet*, *Antony and Cleopatra* and *Troilus and Cressida*.
- The story tells of how that protagonist, the tragic hero, moves from a position of nobility and respect to disgrace and death.
- Often there is an evil character, a villain, to corrupt or oppose the central character: Claudius in *Hamlet* or Iago in *Othello*. Macbeth becomes his own villain, but is corrupted by the witches and (though she wishes him to prosper) his wife.
- Sometimes fate works against the tragic hero, e.g. the prophecy in *Macbeth*.
- The tragedies deal seriously with important subjects like power, love, ambition, madness and many others.
- At the end of a Shakespearean tragedy, after all the deaths, something approaching normality returns, often with a new responsible ruler.

KEY POINT

Several of Shakespeare's tragic heroes are evil or unbalanced or become mad during the play. To some extent, we continue to sympathise with their points of view. This is partly through the use of soliloquies, in which they share their thoughts with the audience.

SEE ALSO Soliloquy, Shakespeare, William (1564–1616), Shakespeare: characters

Verbs

Verbs are often described as 'doing words', but this is only partially correct. Most are verbs of doing and you should have no difficulty in recognising them as verbs: 'shout', 'attack', 'compete' and 'fly' are all very active-sounding, but words like 'sleep', 'rest' and 'wait' are just as much verbs of doing.

However, there are also **verbs of being**. The most common is the verb 'to be', which is the most irregular of all verbs. Other verbs of being include 'become' and 'seem'. A verb of being needs a final part of the sentence to tell us something about the subject: 'He is tall', 'She seemed nervous', 'They were outside the hall'. Interestingly, the verb 'to appear' can be a verb of doing or being. Look at these examples:

'The teacher suddenly appeared.' (doing) 'He appeared very angry.' (being)

Without verbs you cannot build a proper sentence or even make sense. Obviously, in conversation we don't always use proper sentences and sometimes answers make sense because of what has already been said. If you ask, 'Who wrote *Animal Farm*?', then 'George Orwell' makes sense as a reply despite the lack of a verb, but the answer has 'borrowed' the verb 'wrote' from the previous question. You need to distinguish between two forms of verb:

- **Finite verbs.** It is perhaps easier to think of these as main verbs. There is at least one of these in every sentence. They take a subject (the person or object who does the verb) and have a tense (a time when it happens):
  'The class (subject) sits quietly.' (present)
  'I (subject) finished my homework early.' (past)
  'The cup final (subject) will take place in May.' (future)
- **Participles.** Present participles always end in '-ing' and past participles usually end in '-ed', '-t' or '-en'. Despite their names, they do not refer to one time only.
  'He was running.' (present participle referring to the past)
  'We are beaten.' (past participle referring to the present)
  Participles are used with other verbs to make a main verb (as in the two examples just given) or can be used as adjectives, e.g. 'the murdered man' or 'the exploding shell'. What they cannot do is follow a subject on their own to make a sentence: 'He running' does not make sense.

One difficulty with verbs is that often, but not always, the past tense and the past participle are the same, so you say, 'I knocked at the door' (past tense) and 'He was knocked out' (past participle). When they are different, you have to be very careful to use the right one: 'He did well', not 'He done well' or 'She's fallen over', not 'She's fell over'.

SEE ALSO Clauses and phrases, Sentences

45

Writing

Much of what you have to do in English involves writing at some length. Various other sections deal in more detail with aspects of writing, but here are a few generalisations about successful writing:

- Writing is communication. Your first task is to communicate whatever you want (ideas, story, explanation) to whoever your audience is.
- Therefore, the first requirements from your writing are clarity and accuracy (spelling and punctuation), but you should also vary your writing according to what you are trying to communicate.
- You need to be able to write in personal and impersonal styles and to vary the register.
- Be prepared, within reason, to take risks. Use your imagination, try out words you have found in the dictionary. Then learn from both your successes and your mistakes.
- Organisation (including paragraphing) is always important, but avoid being predictable. Try organising a story so that there are frequent shifts of time or it's all in the thoughts of the main character.
- Be ready to explain if necessary. In an essay dealing with ideas or with literature, it is not enough to state an opinion with no evidence.

SEE ALSO Autobiography, Diaries, First and third person, Letters, formal, Letters, informal, Narrative writing, Paragraphs